GORLESTO
SOUTHT
AT THE MOUTH C

Space in this booklet does not allow a full account of the history of Southtown and Gorleston from the early years. The following pages are therefore principally concerned with only the last 200 years, important years for both settlements. Within this period Southtown has developed as a residential area to the west of the main highway, and an industrial area fronting the river. Gorleston has emerged from the fishing village of previous centuries to become a holiday resort in its own right and, particularly during the last 50 years, an important residential area within the Borough of Great Yarmouth.

SOUTHTOWN

In the early years of the 17th century the land on the west bank of the river Yare which made up the hamlet of Southtown belonged to the Paston family. The few houses grouped at the bridge foot housed *"idle and disorderly persons, who spent their time drinking...criminals lurking here awaiting a passage to the continent,"* to quote C J Palmer the 19th century Yarmouth historian. At this time there was no jurisdiction over the area and people lived there *"in utter contempt of their authority"*. After much petitioning to clear up this rather embarrassing neighbourhood a charter was obtained from Charles II in 1668 to unite Yarmouth with Southtown or Little Yarmouth as it

The Haven Bridge 1854-1928. The vital river crossing from Yarmouth to Southtown and Gorleston. This was the sixth bridge across the river Yare at this point.

was also known. The inhabitants now came under the laws, taxes and government of the town, although for ecclesiastical purposes Southtown remained in the parish of Gorleston. Shortly after this Sir Robert Paston published proposals to build a new town along the riverside with new quays and substantial houses. No one appears to have been interested enough to invest in this ambitious scheme and it was to be another 100 years before a demand for houses on the west side of the river materialised.

By 1734 ownership of the land had passed to Commodore Anson, a sea captain who had circumnavigated the world. The 700 acres of Southtown stretched along the river bank from the Lady Haven stream which divided it from Cobholm Island to the Gorleston boundary. Until the 1891 county boundary revisions the river formed the boundary between Norfolk and Suffolk, both Southtown and Gorleston then being in a different county to their administrative centre.

The main London road passed through Southtown, beginning at the Yarmouth bridge. It was at one time a lonely and notorious stretch of highway across marsh and bog, many people preferring to enter and leave Yarmouth by the Gorleston ferry to avoid the highway. In 1748 a man was hanged for a robbery committed on the Southtown Road. By the latter part of the 18th century the road was described as *"being in a ruinous condition and unsafe for passengers"* which resulted in the Parliamentary Act of 1774 to make it a Turnpike road. Toll-bars collected the dues from travellers, these going towards the expense of keeping the road in reasonable repair. The Act was repealed in 1875.

Bridge Road, Southtown, in the 1920s. The tram at the terminus ready to leave for Gorleston.

From the beginning of the 19th century many Great Yarmouth merchants chose the west side of the river as a site to build their private residences. A line of handsome houses began to appear on the western side of the Southtown Turnpike, the land between the road and river being used for ship-building yards, wharves, timber yards and other industrial purposes.

Many of the large houses built along the west side of the Turnpike had unusual 'crinkle-crankle' or undulating garden walls, fashionable in the period 1780 to 1820. Their function, apart from the visual appeal, was to protect fruit trees, but in a marshy area such as Southtown they also had the advantage of being self-buttressing. Youell, the Yarmouth diarist, recorded in 1807 *"I was at my new house [on Southtown Road opposite the Armoury] when they began to build the Serpentine Wall."* Sections of these walls that still survive are considered interesting enough to be listed, being of architectural and historical importance. Among the early residents of Southtown were Robert Steward, the first person to be elected mayor on three consecutive occasions; Lieut Orfeur RN; John Sell Cotman, the 19th century painter; Captain William Manby, renowned for his inventions which included life saving apparatus; and Sir Edmund Lacon, the brewer.

The fire at Clarke's flour mill and Jewson's wood yard on 2nd June 1928, from the Yarmouth side of the river. The port tug 'George Jewson' is assisting the fire brigade. The fire burned for two days.

This early development was summed up by another Yarmouth historian, John Greaves Nall, who wrote in 1867 *"at the present day Southtown contains many neat and commodious private residences and forms an agreeable suburb of Yarmouth."*

The church of St Mary's Southtown was built in 1831 to serve the increasing population, on land given by the Earl of Lichfield. Later several terraces of houses comprising Bunns Lane, St Mary's Lane and Sefton Lane were built around the church. To the rear of the large houses on the western side of the main road the Lichfield Estate was commenced in the 1890s after a pumping station had been built to drain the marshy ground. Until well into this century cattle sales were held every Wednesday at the saleground in Station Road, established in 1892. Another saleground was situated just to the west of the Two Bears Hotel, the cattle sales having moved to Southtown from Priory Plain at the northern end of Great Yarmouth Market Place.

In 1812 the Southtown 'High Mill' was built for Thomas Woolsey. With a height of 122 feet and sail span of 84 feet this 12 storey mill was claimed to be the highest in England, the four pairs of mill-stones capable of crushing 30 cwt of oats per hour. A roadway passed through the base of the mill enabling carts to load and unload within the mill itself. In 1854 the mill came into national prominence during the Crimean War when flour was supplied to Lord Raglans's army, carried from Great Yarmouth in clipper schooners to the Black Sea ports. The last owner of the High Mill was Mr B H Press and on his death in 1904 it was sold by auction for £100, then demolished and the bricks used to build a terrace of houses. The exact site of the mill is marked by red chimney pots on numbers 35 and 36 Gatacre Road.

Another well known Southtown mill was Green Cap or Hammond's Mill which stood where Century Road now runs. This mill was destroyed by fire in January 1898. Towards the end of the 19th century the work of the windmills was taken over by the new steam powered mills, one of this type being erected in what became Steam Mill Lane.

Great Yarmouth was without a Grammar School between the years 1757 and 1863 and to fill this educational gap several private schools opened, one of which was the Great Yarmouth Proprietary Grammar School built in 1834 on a site near the bridge foot, not far from the Bear Inn. In 1850 this was classed as the town's principal school *"catering for 100 sons and relatives of gentlemen, merchants and the most respected inhabitants of the town. The head master is a clergyman and in every respect it is an establishment of a superior character."* In 1858 the school buildings were demolished and the following year a railway goods yard, connected to Southtown Station, stood on the site. It is now a 'Do It All' DIY store.

Timber yards lined the west bank of the river for over 100 years. In 1880 Jewson and Sons, Thomas Saul and Son, and Joshua Ranson were among the first companies to import large quantities of timber from Russia and Scandinavia. Palgrave Brown and Orfeur and Bellin joined Jewsons as the main companies involved in this trade. Today two of these importers have gone, the large storage sheds that once dominated the area either being demolished or put to other uses.

For centuries the river Yare has been an important ship building area and on the west bank of the river the first yard was established in 1785 by Isaac Preston. The early years of the 19th century were boom years for the yards and in 1818 nearly 100 vessels were built in 12 months along the river banks. Preston's yard was taken over by Henry Fellows early in the century, and 100 years later it was taken over by F T Everard and Son who sold it to Richards of Lowestoft in 1970. This is now the only shipyard on the river.

Also on the west bank was the yard of T Saul and Co, a site later becoming Clarkes Flour Mill, John Rust's yard and Bessey and Palmers yard next to J and H Bunn's premises. Between this and Fellows was the yard of Mills and Blake, who built sailing coasters, a yard taken over by Crabtree and Co, who built many steel drifters. J Mack and Son and Samuel Seago also had shipyards in this area and these later became the site for the large timber sheds of Palgrave Brown and Son.

Midway along Southtown Road, on a site between the road and the river a naval arsenal was built in 1806. When completed the armoury contained arms to equip 10,000 troops, two frigates, six sloops and two ships of the line. This was at a period when the town played an important role in supporting the navy, ships anchoring in the Roads to take on supplies and men. Officers' quarters and a chapel were built facing Southtown Road. After the Napoleonic Wars had come to an end the remaining arms were transferred to London and deposited in the Tower. In 1835 the Southtown buildings were converted into Militia Barracks for the Norfolk Militia Artillery. In 1871 the Prince of Wales (later King Edward VII) dined with members of the Regiment at the Southtown Barracks. In 1891 the buildings were acquired by J and J Colman Ltd, the mustard company, for warehouses and were used by that firm until the wharf and riverside buildings were severely damaged by bombing in 1942. Today some of the buildings still exist, now used by companies connected with the oil industry. The cannon that stands at the north end of Great Yarmouth Market Place was excavated from this site in 1982 and is an example of the 18th century hardware stored at the armoury for the British Fleet.

Towards the southern end of Southtown Road, on a site adjacent to the river, the Gorleston and Southtown Gas Light and Coke Co Ltd built a works in 1855 to supply the inhabitants of the area with gas. By 1928 the British Gas Light Co had taken over and the following year the works were rebuilt and modernised. Although bombed by a Zeppelin in 1915, hit 14 times the following year by bombardment from the sea and bombed again in 1941, the gas works continued to produce coal gas until June 1965. The works were demolished two years later and the gasholders in 1974; the site is today used by oil companies.

Ferryside, from 1972 the Registrar's Office and Gorleston Fire Station, was, at the beginning of the 19th century, the site of a boys' boarding school known as the Southtown Academy for Young Gentlemen. In 1880 a new house was built on the site by Edward Harvey Combe, a maltster, and large malthouses were built in the northern part of the grounds. To the east, separated by Malthouse Lane, were some earlier malthouses built in the mid-18th century by Whitbreads. These were taken over by Combe in 1888 and a few years later the Corporation granted permission for a bridge to be built across the lane to connect the two maltings. Later these all became part of a large complex owned by Watney, Combe and Reid, later known as Watney Mann. In 1976 the quayside buildings and the bridge were demolished. The main maltings continued for a few more years. The house, Ferryside, was occupied by Dr Willis before the war and in 1947 the Corporation purchased it for use as a children's home. In 1960 it was taken over by the Welfare Services and Children's Department.

From 1941 fire engines were stationed on the site and in 1944 a purpose built fire station was erected, the firemen living in the house until 1947. During the time the fire service was under the control of the National Fire Service a fire-boat was stationed at the adjacent quay.

GORLESTON

Gorleston, originally a small fishing and farming community on the high ground overlooking the mouth of the river Yare, was added to the Borough of Great Yarmouth in 1832, a result of the Parliamentary and Municipal Reform Act. By the mid-19th century it was still a small settlement, indeed the combined population of Gorleston and Southtown was still below 4,000 with only 948 houses. The houses of Gorleston were strung out along the High Street, Baker Street, Pier Plain and Cliff Hill, with a few houses grouped around the White Horse road junction, to the west of which were the lands of Ottey's Farm and to the south, Hammond's Farm. Between Pier Plain and the river were marshes and from Feathers Plain a narrow lane, Church Lane, led to the parish church of St Andrew. What was later to become Englands Lane was a track to Palmer's Farm and to the south of this, extending inland from the cliff edge, were Barber's Farm and Crowe's

Fishers Institute, used in 1910 as auction rooms, was demolished to make way for the Coliseum Cinema. The cart belongs to Bloomfield's, the marquee hire firm.

Hammond's shop on the corner of Lowestoft Road and Church Lane, about 1905. Bassinettes were a type of wicker baby carriage.

Farm. From this it can be seen that Gorleston was bounded on the west and south by extensive agricultural lands, cows roaming over much of what today are thickly populated built-up areas. Fishing was dovetailed with the farming, many field gates and fences made from timbers of broken-up smacks and many farm workers turning to the fishing industry during the herring season. Gorleston's association with farming may be the reason why the Suffolk Agricultural Show was held there in 1913, a special railway siding being built for the wagons that brought the exhibits to the show.

In 1865 a new road, Priory Street, was built to connect High Street to Church Road. On the south side of Priory Street a Drill Hall was erected in 1875 for the Gorleston contingent of the 2nd Norfolk Volunteers, a building that was later used for public entertainment and meetings. The supply of fresh drinking water in Gorleston was improved in 1872 when the Yarmouth Water Company constructed a covered reservoir off the Lowestoft Road to hold 800,000 gallons of water pumped from Ormesby Broad, a reservoir that is still in use today.

The population began to rise towards the end of the century and by 1881 about 6,000 people lived in Gorleston, although when Cook published his Directory of Yarmouth and Gorleston in 1886 it was only considered necessary to list the five 'principal streets' of Baker Street, Cliff Hill, High Street, Pier Plain and Pier Walk. Towards the end of the century Upper Cliff, Lower Cliff, Nelson and Bells Roads were laid out on open land previously owned by John Sayers Bell.

During the First World War many buildings in Baker Street and Riverside Road were occupied by the Royal Navy as a shore base called *HMS Kingfisher*. In 1916 a 4.7 inch gun was installed on the cliff, on the upper esplanade, midway between Clarence Road and Park Road, to overlook and defend the harbour. The Cliff Hotel burnt down in a disastrous fire on Boxing Day 1915 when it was under naval occupation, and the estimated cost of rebuilding was £30,000.

During the winter of 1922/23 a new and important road was constructed to link Gorleston church with the Lowestoft Road at Elmhurst, namely Middleton Road. Ten years later a roundabout, the first to be built in the Borough, was made at the Church Lane junction. With the construction of this road Gorleston began to spread westwards and in 1932 the Corporation purchased 958 acres of land from Magdalen College Oxford for £35,000, eventually to be developed as the Magdalen Estate. The 1930s were years of expansion for Gorleston and in 1930 a new housing development was started on the cliffs, much of this being related to the popularity of the town as a holiday resort. Further land was purchased for the Magdalen Estate in 1938 and a limited amount of development took place in the immediate pre-war years.

The Second World War saw more military occupation of Gorleston and in 1941 the Links Battery was constructed at the end of Marine Parade on the Borough boundary. Two 6-inch guns, with underground shelters and magazines, and two searchlights, were installed. The surrounding bungalows provided the quarters for the personnel who manned the battery; some buildings were used as stores, some as living accommodation and one as the officers' mess. The armament was later increased with two 40mm Bofors guns and a 25-pounder field gun. The battery was manned until January 1945.

Following the destruction of housing in Great Yarmouth during the war the need to build new homes in the Borough dramatically increased and in 1944 the Housing Committee looked to the Magdalen Estate to provide up to 1350 new homes for people displaced from the Row and Middlegate areas of the town. In September 1944 it was announced that all local authorities

The White Lion
Hotel and steps
about 1910.

were to be supplied with a number of prefabricated houses to speed up the re-housing programme. A site of 60 acres was acquired at the west end of Gorleston cemetery, near Shrublands Farm, for the new 'prefabs'. The following year this was officially designated the Shrublands Estate, all the roads being named after flowering shrubs, and work progressed on the site, the smaller part of which was south of Crabb Lane (Laburnum Road) and the larger part of the estate between Crabb Lane and Beccles Road. Much of the site preparation work was carried out by German prisoners-of-war, the first buildings being delivered in January 1946. By the time the 711 homes were completed it had become the largest prefab estate in the country, the weekly rent being 12s 6d (62p). The buildings were originally designed to last for 10 years but most were not demolished until the latter part of the 1960s to make way for more permanent housing. There was another, much smaller, development of prefabs in Bells Marsh Road.

The north side of Church Lane in the 1890s.

The first phase of development on the Magdalen Estate commenced in 1946 with 120 houses and continued the following year with another 55 homes. It was decided that the theme for the road names would be the Colleges of Oxford and Cambridge Universities and in 1948 some long established road names were changed. Cemetery Lane became Magdalen Way and part of Long Lane became Trinity Avenue. More land was released for the estate in 1948 when the Council decided not to retain land it had reserved for a western by-pass as it considered the existing road system through Gorleston could be widened and improved to meet all future needs, a decision now proved to have been wrong.

In 1948 another housing development commenced when land became available in the area bounded by Marine Parade, Bridge Road and Arnott Avenue, being called the Cliff Park Estate. In 1951 the population had risen to 17,900 and was expected to increase to over 25,000 during the following 20 years and to this end the development of the Magdalen Estate continued in the 1950s with about 300 houses being completed each year.

Gorleston had now become the residential area for neighbouring Great Yarmouth. Work was available on the South Denes industrial area which continued to expand throughout the 1950s and 1960s, and it was within easy commuting distance using the ferry.

THE TRAMWAY

On 25th March 1875 the East Suffolk Tramway Company opened a three mile horse-drawn tramway connecting Southtown Station with Gorleston Feathers Plain. This early system was built to a 4ft 8inch gauge but seven years later it was taken over by the newly formed Yarmouth and Gorleston Tramway Co Ltd and the tracks were relaid to the more conventional 3ft 6inch gauge. The new owners extended the service via Lowestoft Road and Englands Lane to a terminus near the King William IV public house on

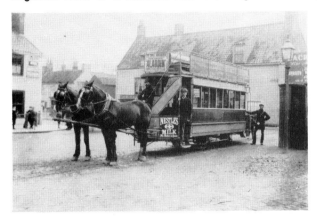

A horse tram at the Feathers Plain terminus in 1897.

An electric tram in Gorleston High Street. Bussey's grocers shop is on the right of the picture.

Brush Quay. After the company had obtained shares in the Yarmouth and Gorleston Steamboat Co Ltd it was possible to buy a 6d return ticket that allowed passengers to travel out from Southtown by tram and return by steamboat to Hall Quay. The journey from Southtown to Gorleston could take up to one hour to complete and it was said that a good walker could arrive at Feathers Plain before the tram. For part of the journey along Lowestoft Road an additional horse, referred to as a 'trace' or 'tip' horse was hitched to the tram to assist the two regular horses up the incline. This extra horse-power was also required during periods of snow and ice along other sections of the route.

Between 70 and 80 horses were stabled at the Feathers Plain depot and these were used to pull the ten double deck horse-trams and the seven horse buses that provided the Gorleston service. In 1905 the Yarmouth Corporation took over the Tramway Company and within six months, using a workforce exceeding 600 men, had relaid and extended the tracks and electrified the system.

The 'tip' or 'trace' horse helping to pull a tram up the incline at the junction of England's Lane and Lowestoft Road in 1897.

The last horse tram was driven to the Yareside Ironworks on Southtown Road where wedges were put in the rails and the tram car pulled off the track. The new electric tramway opened on July 4th 1905 with a civic party travelling on three decorated trams followed by a lunch at the Cliff Hotel.

From Feathers Plain one track ran via Lowestoft Road to the railway station and another, via Baker Street, Pier Plain and Brush Quay, to a terminus outside the Pavilion, the Gorleston Beach route. The old horse-tram route via Englands Lane was abandoned due to the cost of widening the roadway. A new depot was erected at Feathers Plain beside the old one. These buildings remained, largely unused, until demolished to make way for the new Library which opened on the site in 1974.

The Gorleston tramway system could not be linked with the Great Yarmouth system, the Haven Bridge not being suitable to carry the tracks. The terminus was moved from Southtown Station to a point nearer the bridge in Bridge Road and the fare was 1d to the half-way stage and 2d to the Gorleston termini. In 1924 a motor bus service commenced from the Britannia Pier to Gorleston and for the first time a public transport system crossed the river. The last electric tram ran on the Gorleston system on 25th September 1930, replaced by a Yarmouth to Gorleston bus service.

THE RAILWAY

Yarmouth Southtown station opened on June 1st 1859 as the terminus for the East Suffolk line. This was a major route between Yarmouth and London via Beccles with express, local and freight traffic. Holiday traffic on this line rapidly increased until, by 1871, over 35,000 people were arriving at Southtown each year by excursion trains alone. A line was laid across the Southtown Road to connect with a goods yard, the goods lines extending to the river where a series of turntables allowed the trucks to be turned at right angles along the river frontage and past the ice houses (only one of which remains today).

A steam train leaving Gorleston station bound for Yarmouth Southtown in the 1950s.

Another local rail service from Southtown commenced on July 13th 1903 when the Norfolk and Suffolk Joint Railway, an arrangement between the GER and the M & GN railways, opened a coastal line to Lowestoft. This was quickly followed later that year by a link to Yarmouth Beach via the new Breydon Swing Bridge. This line was designed to serve the rapidly developing holiday areas along the stretch of coast south of Yarmouth and also to obtain for the company a share in the lucrative fish trade from Lowestoft. 24 acres of land were purchased in Gorleston for the new line and two stations, Gorleston and Gorleston North were built. The station at

Gorleston North, the entrance being a slope from the north side of Burgh Road, soon became an important coal depot, supplying coal to the steam drifter fleets. Gorleston Links Halt was built in 1914 to serve the Gorleston golf club.

The main Gorleston station, with the ticket office at Victoria Road level, was built in a cutting and the platforms were reached by a slope, a footbridge linking the up and down platforms. A goods shed, coal yard and cattle pens were situated to the west of the main line, the coal depot being used by four firms - Bessey and Palmer, Thomas Moy, Guyton and Read and Bert Raywood. The extensive sidings were used to store coaches which in the 1950s and 1960s made up the Holiday Camp Specials. These trains started at Gorleston and picked up passengers at the coastal holiday camps between there and Lowestoft, then travelling through to London.

The station at Gorleston North was damaged by bombing in 1942 and did not reopen. The same year Southtown Station narrowly escaped serious damage when a bomb fell on the tracks but did not explode, being quickly defused by a member of the Bomb Disposal Squad who happened to be at the station at the time. The floods of 1953 caused a serious problem, no trains being able to run in or out for a week. In 1959 the line to Beccles closed, and the direct link to London was lost. The coastal line was upgraded and for a few years the London trains ran via Lowestoft, but in 1962 all London trains were diverted to Yarmouth Vauxhall, a pay train service then being provided to Lowestoft. The main buildings at Southtown were let to an oil company for office accommodation. The last train ran on the line in May 1970 and the buildings at Southtown were finally demolished in 1977 to clear the way for Pasteur Road.

THE RIVERSIDE

Lifeboats have been associated with Gorleston since the mid-19th century and today the station forms an important link in the coastal rescue service provided by the RNLI. Located so close to the mouth of the Yarmouth haven, Gorleston has always been in an ideal position. The 19th century boatmen found plenty of work, not only in salvage and rescue but also as pilots taking vessels up to the Yarmouth quays and working further afield guiding ships through the treacherous sand banks and channels off the coast. The beachmen moved into houses on Cliff Hill, overlooking the harbour, forming a separate 'beach community'. Early in the century these beachmen had organised themselves into groups or 'companies', as had their compatriots in nearly all the towns and villages along the East Anglian coastline. The Gorleston companies were known as the Storm, the Ranger and the Young Flies, and with their yawls, lifeboats and smaller boats they assisted vessels in trouble, making their living from the salvage work which was plentiful at that period due to poor navigation and the badly maintained boats that plied along the east coast.

The Ranger and Storm companies were probably formed in the 1820s while the Young Flies did not materialise until 1863. Each company had their own headquarters and look-out tower from which they could keep watch in bad weather. Competition was fierce as the rewards from salvage could be considerable. The Ranger and Storm companies worked from look-outs near the Anchor and Hope public house at the foot of the pier until the 1860s when they moved to buildings on Brush Quay. The Young Flies look-out was built onto the roof of the building adjoining the William the Fourth public house, and until recent years a lookout tower survived on the roof of the building now known as the Storm House Cafe.

There have been many lifeboats stationed at Gorleston, some privately owned by the boatmen mentioned above, others by the RNLI. The earliest lifeboat was the *Rescuer*, owned by the Ranger Company and built by the Yarmouth boat builder Beeching in 1855. In 1857 the Storm Company had a lifeboat called the *Refuge*, a boat which in 1881 was bought by the newly formed Gorleston Voluntary Lifeboat Association. They then chose the Ranger Company to run it for them until 1888 when it was replaced by what has probably become the most well-known Gorleston lifeboat, the *Elizabeth Simpson*, also built by Beeching. The *Elizabeth Simpson's* story is told in a companion book in this series. The Young Flies Company also owned a lifeboat, the *Friend of All Nations*, built in 1863.

The RNLI, more interested in lifesaving than salvage, established a station at Gorleston in 1866, partly as a result of a disaster in January that year when the Ranger Company's boat *Rescuer* overturned in the harbour and 12 of the crew were drowned. The first RNLI lifeboat was the *Leicester*, replaced in 1870 by another boat of the same name. A No 2 station was operational from 1883 until 1924, its three lifeboats saving 205 lives, a No 3 station worked from 1892 until 1904 and a No 4 station from 1897 until 1908. The closure of the Yarmouth lifeboat station in 1919 increased the workload of the Gorleston station, although the introduction of the first motor lifeboat, the *John and Mary Meiklam*, in 1924 meant there was only a need for one lifeboat from that time. From 1963 an inshore lifeboat has been stationed at Gorleston and in 1967 the first of a new American-style steel hulled boat, the *Khami*, took over the rescue work. This boat was replaced in 1980 with the *Barham* which today continues the long tradition of lifesaving from the Gorleston station.

The lifeboats of both the RNLI and the private companies were housed in a row of riverside boathouses, some of which still stand. The earliest was built for the Ranger Company in 1855 and adjacent to that was the boathouse of the Volunteer Lifeboat. The modern lifeboat is kept afloat, in a small dock, near the old buildings.

THE GORLESTON WHALE

There are many stories which can be told of the Gorleston fishing community. Limitation of space means that only one can be included here. On Monday 8th June 1891 a whale got itself lost among the many sandbanks and shallow waters off the harbour mouth and eventually, with the help of an incoming tide, ended up in the harbour. It became entangled in the wooden piles of the piers injuring itself, and as the tide fell the animal was stranded.

A small fleet of boats put out after the whale and managed to get some ropes fixed to it. The Gorleston lifeboatmen then killed it. A chain was put round the tail and it was towed towards the lifeboat sheds where, with the aid of a winch, it was hauled into the Volunteer Lifeboat House which usually housed the *Elizabeth Simpson* lifeboat. It was identified as a Lesser Rorqual whale, 35 feet long, having a girth of 18 feet and a tail span of eight feet, the length of the jaws being six feet six inches.

The Gorleston beachmen and their whale in 1891.

After being exhibited to the public for a short time it became necessary to decide the long term future of what had become a useful source of income for the beachmen. The local veterinary surgeon, Mr Shipley, was called in to dissect it. With the help of the lifeboatmen this unpleasant task was completed with some difficulty, the smell being so strong that tar was burnt in the shed to counteract it. Considerable difficulty was experienced in removing the internal organs of the animal and while this was being done, in the presence of a large crowd, the local naturalist Arthur Patterson (or John

15

Knowlittle as he was perhaps better known) gave a lecture on the history of whales. A local taxidermist, Walter Lowne, then undertook the task of preserving the carcase for £30 and after a rough skinning the fat lined hide was taken to his loft on Fullers Hill where several weeks were spent scraping away the blubber and pickling the skin in a solution of nitrate of soda. Iron hoops were made and the skin fitted round them, the inside being stuffed with straw and other material and a large wooden backbone fitted until it finally resembled the original shape of the whale.

A long trailer was built to carry the stuffed whale and it was taken to London to be exhibited at Westminster Aquarium, a favourite venue for such things. The whale was then brought to Norwich where it was exhibited for two weeks before moving to Lowestoft for a further fortnight. Following this it was brought back to Great Yarmouth for the summer season. After this the whale took to the road again and travelled the country with various showmen. In the course of these travels the skin became badly moth-eaten and damaged. The showmen repaired the damage with painted brown paper, so much so that towards the end of its exhibition career those who paid to see it saw more painted paper than whale! What was left of the exhibit ended its days back at Great Yarmouth, the bones finally being ground up for fertilizer.

FISHING INDUSTRY

Gorleston played an important role in the Yarmouth herring fishing industry in the second part of the 19th century. The Short Blue Fleet, of over 220 fishing smacks owned by the Hewitt family and based at Barking on the Thames, moved part of their business to Gorleston in 1865. The spread of the railways and the need to find new fishing grounds were the main reasons for the move. The firm built their own shipyard, dry dock and ice house on a four acre site at the foot of what became known as Ice House Hill. Tunnels leading into the hill were used for storing salt, ice and tar, and a hostel was built for the smack boys next to Captain Manby's house in High Road. Cottages for the workers and their families, known as Hewitts Buildings, were built off the High Street, Hewitt's Score leading from High Street to the company wharf. The cottage hospital in Trafalgar Road was largely paid for by the company.

The business had originated in 1764 and the name was taken from the square blue flag flown on all the company smacks. By the end of the century the majority of the fleet had moved from Barking to Gorleston and the company had become one of the town's main employers. In 1889 the building known as the Tower in High Street was built for Harvey George, company manager, and from here the fleet could be seen returning to port and prior arrangements made for berthing and unloading. Sail was giving way to steam and by 1901 the company had closed its original Thames base and concentrated on Gorleston, but by 1905 its operations had become seriously affected by steam trawling and it had started to reduce its fleet and dispose of its Gorleston property. The subsequent withdrawal of the Hewitt Fleet had a serious impact on Gorleston, almost 4000 people having relied upon it for work and housing. Two public houses, the Barking Fishery and the Short Blue, were later named after the company.

BRUSH QUAY

The length of quay from the lifeboat sheds to the South Pier is known as Brush Quay. It takes its name from the Brush Bend where the river was diverted at right angles to form the harbour's mouth, the diversion being achieved by blocking the old river course with soil and brushwood. This diversion of the river and the associated construction of the north and south piers to form the seventh Yarmouth Haven were masterminded by a Dutchman, Joyce Johnson, brought to the town in the 16th century to solve once and for all Yarmouth's problems in achieving a stable harbour entrance. In the 1950s the north pier was reconstructed and in the 1960s extensive works were necessary on the 400 year old timbers of the south

Brush Quay, about 1880. The original William IV public house can be seen in the top left of the picture, beside the meadow that later became known as Pops Meadow.

The 'cosies' on the old south pier. The coastguard station is at the end of the pier.

pier. The popular 'cosies' or alcoves where many generations of locals and visitors had sat to watch the shipping were removed. At the end of the south pier was the Coastguard lookout and midway along the pier stood the

The end of the old south pier was a popular spot for fishing or just watching the shipping.

The new south pier was started in March 1962 and finished in February 1964. This picture was taken in August 1962 after a gale had smashed down part of the new piling.

wooden capstan, which was used for many years to assist sailing vessels to enter the harbour. The lighthouse was erected on the Bend in 1887 by the Port and Haven Commissioners to assist navigation.

For many years a steamer service ran from Brush Quay to Great Yarmouth Town Hall, the boats being owned by the Yarmouth and Gorleston Steamboat Co. One of earliest of these was the *Lily*, the fare in 1901 being adults 2d, children 1d. These double ended boats, built with two sets of controls to avoid the need to turn around in the busy river, were very popular both with visitors and local residents. Later boats had local names such as *Cobholm, Southtown, Yarmouth* and one, the *Resolute*, was preserved at a dry dock in London, forming part of a heritage collection of boats which until recently included the Yarmouth drifter *Lydia Eva*.

HOLIDAY RESORT

Gorleston began to develop as a holiday resort towards the end of the 19th century and in 1898 the Cliff Hotel was built on a prominent site on the cliff top, overlooking the old pier and harbour entrance. In 1889 a sea wall was constructed at the foot of the cliffs and the following year the Council announced a set of regulations covering the Parade, beach and cliffs, prohibiting games such as 'Aunt Sally' and coconut shies. No person was allowed to walk or lie on the cliff slope and begging, hawking, puppet shows and dangerous and noisy games were banned. In 1896 a bandstand, a popular feature in almost every seaside resort, was erected in the gardens near the Pier Hotel. In 1903 the Yarmouth Corporation invested more money in the fast growing holiday area by extending the Marine Parade, erecting shelters and cutting the Ravine through the cliffs as an access to the beach. Gorleston now began to develop away from the old centre around the High Street and expanded to the south, along the cliffs.

Holiday entertainment in the form of concert parties and pierrot groups played at the Pavilion and on the cliffs, where in 1904 Uncle Walter's Pierrots performed. The bathing machines, another essential seaside facility, first appeared at Gorleston in the 1890s, owned by the Capps family. Grandfather Capps, as the founder of the business was known, ran 13 single machines and four 'family' machines. A single machine cost 3d per person and included the use of a towel and bathing dress. The family machines were double width with two doors on the landward side and a single door leading to the water. Swimming lessons were also given by Mr Capps two sons, William Isaac Capps and Whitmore Capps. The strict 19th century regulations connected with bathing from the beach had been relaxed by this time and mixed bathing had become acceptable. During the winter months these machines were stored near the lighthouse.

Capps bathing machines on Gorleston beach, about 1900. 'Whitey' Capps can be seen advertising his 13 machines for 3d per session.

Other machines soon appeared on the beach as did tents and refreshment stalls. A visitor in the early years of the 20th century said of Gorleston "...*a rising watering-place that at first sight impresses one as being a typical example of those small modern coastal resorts which owe their existence to the enterprise of the speculative builder. Its sea front with its zigzag cliff footpaths, its ornamental shelters, its upper and lower esplanades, is strikingly new, and its big hotel and monotonous terraces are especially indicative of recently attained popularity."*

The Pavilion, or Shelter Hall as it was also known, was first proposed at a Borough Council meeting in 1897 to meet the demands of the expanding holiday resort and, despite comments such as *"the housing of the working classes is far more important than a Shelter Hall at Gorleston"* and *"the time is hardly ripe for expenditure of £6,000"* from some councillors, the building work progressed as planned and it was opened in July 1901. The design was by the Borough Surveyor, J W Cockrill, (responsible for shaping both Yarmouth and Gorleston as holiday resorts) and in 1919 a sliding roof was installed above the main hall, this surviving until blown away by a gale in 1950s.

In June 1919 a meadow near the William IV public house, belonging to Miss Mary Baumgartner of Cliff Hill, was leased by Henry Clay who erected a marquee in which his 'Gorleston Pops' concert party performed for the summer season. Clay had provided entertainment with his 'Musical Party' during the 1913 and 1914 seasons at the Pavilion, returning to Gorleston

Steamboat trips from Yarmouth to Gorleston were popular at the turn of the century. This is the booking office on Hall Quay.

The Cliff Hotel was built in 1898 and burnt down in 1915. In the foreground are the gardens and bandstand, removed to build the Floral Hall (now the Ocean Rooms).

Visitors and residents alike joined the celebrations for the 1897 Jubilee. An ox was roasted on Brush quay. The gentleman in the top hat is the Rev. Forbes Phillips, Vicar of Gorleston from 1893 to 1917. In uniform is Colonel Combe, the maltster who lived at Ferryside.

after the war. In 1925 the marquee was replaced by a wooden Concert Hall, built by a local boatbuilder and this was used for 'Henry Clay's Pops' until 1934 when the council refused to renew the licence unless a brick building replaced the wooden structure. The Concert Hall was demolished and Mr Clay left Gorleston, the open piece of land, part of which is now a putting course, always being referred to as 'Pops Meadow'.

On August Bank Holiday Monday 1912 both residents and visitors were given a chance to view at close hand the latest wonder of the age, a flying machine. A young aviator, Bentfield C Hucks, made the first recorded flight by an aeroplane over Norfolk when he flew his Bleriot monoplane, called *Firefly*, from a field at Crow Hall farm to Eaton near Norwich. The Eastern Daily Press reported that the machine, powered by a 75hp Gnome engine, *"...sent a thrill of excitement through the crowd"*. Gorleston was again in the aviation news in 1931 when A W Fairlie made the first recorded parachute jump in Norfolk at the Gorleston Air Show.

The first cinema to open in Gorleston was Filmland in Beach Road on July 21st 1913. This was also known as The Playhouse, Scala and, by 1927, The Palace. The building closed before the Second World War and was later destroyed by an air raid. Only a month after Filmland opened its doors another cinema, the Coliseum, opened on August Bank Holiday 1914. The Coliseum Buildings, extending along the High Street to Palmer Road, consisted of a provision shop, a fruit shop, the Maypole Dairy, Smiths Cleaners and the picture house itself, built on land that had been part of Rope's farm. The cinema remained open until January 1970 when it was demolished to make way for a new shopping development. Another cinema called The Palace opened in the High Street in 1939 but in 1964 it was converted to a Bingo Hall.

A late 1920s view of the Coliseum cinema foyer. A notice says 'Silence is essential for the full enjoyment of talking pictures'.

The 1937 Great Yarmouth holiday guide described Gorleston as *"a resort for discerning holidaymakers"* and the beach, of which Gorleston was justifiably proud, was described as *"sands of wondrous purity and softness, shelving so gradually that safer bathing could not be imagined"*.

In 1938 the bandstand and gardens were replaced by a dance hall, the Floral Hall, (now the Ocean Rooms) and a swimming pool (demolished in 1993). Another popular 1930s attraction was the model yacht pond.

The beach had been mined in 1940 and after the war never returned to the golden sands of the pre-war era. Shingle and stone built up and in the 1960s the condition of the beach was blamed for the decline in Gorleston's popularity as a seaside resort. Many new hotels and guest houses had opened in the immediate pre-war and post-war years along Marine Parade and adjoining roads, but in more recent times many of these have become nursing homes or retirement accommodation, a trend that has caused many people to become concerned about Gorleston's future as a holiday resort.

THE BREWERY

The Gorleston Brewery, later known as Bells Brewery, was established by William Killett in 1620 on a site towards the eastern end of Baker Street, on the corner of what is now Pier Plain. The Killetts were a prominent family in the town for many years. Samuel Killett, when Mayor in 1746, presented the town with a silver oar, about four feet in length, as a symbol of the town's Admiralty jurisdiction and today this is part of the town's silver collection, kept in the Town Hall.

The family house of the Killett's was built in 1722 and later became a public house known as the Globe Tavern. In the 18th century the brewery business was sold to John Baker, later passing to John Baker Bell and finally to John Sayers Bell. In 1841 Steward, Patteson and Finch secured the lease of 22 public houses in Gorleston belonging to Bell's brewery, and the brewery was then closed. Although the brewery was in business for over 200 years it does not appear to have owned any public houses outside Gorleston, except the Ferry Boat in Southtown. Maltings, workshops and stables were situated on the north side of Baker Street, directly opposite the main brewery buildings. By the 1880s the site had become a sawmill belonging to John Fellows.

John Sayers Bell died in 1851, a member of a family that owned much land in Gorleston and whose name is now recalled by Bells Road.

About 1870 another brewery owned by G C Kew was opened in the High

Street, next door to the Temperance Hall. The conflict of interest between the two buildings must have caused some comment in the late 19th century.

PUBLIC HOUSES

There have been, and still are, many public houses in Southtown and Gorleston. An 1850 Directory lists the following:

SOUTHTOWN	GORLESTON
Angel (or Guardian Angel)	Anchor and Hope
Anson's Arms	Dukes Head
Ferry Boat	Earl Grey
Greyhound	Feathers
Queen's Arms	George and Dragon
Rising Sun	Globe
Rumbold Arms	Red Lion
St Andrew's Hall	Salvage Boat
Three Tuns	Ship
	White Horse
	White Lion
	William IV

The QUEENS ARM'S listed above stood on the corner of Steam Mill Lane, set back from Bridge Road, and later this became the site of the BRIDGE HOTEL. On the opposite side of the road, at the foot of the old bridge, was the BEAR, not listed above because it was demolished in 1849 when the river was widened and construction of the new bridge commenced. This bridge opened in 1854 and was replaced in 1930 with the present structure.

The Bear had stood on this site for many years, the following notice appearing in the Norfolk Chronicle in December 1785

'Notice given on 6th December 1785 at Gt Yarmouth. At the Bear Inn Bridge Foot on 19th December 1785 part of the cargo of the brig *Nancy* will be sold by auction.'

In the early years of the 19th century the London coach left from here three times a week. The Evening Star New Post Coach went to London via Bury every Sunday, Tuesday and Thursday at 3.45pm.

The NEW BRIDGE TAVERN was opened in Steam Mill Lane shortly after 1854, a Lacons house until it was closed in 1926 and the property sold to William Shipley, the veterinary surgeon.

The TWO BEARS (at first called THE BEAR) on the corner of Mill Road opened soon after the Southtown Railway station and was for many years a Morgans house. This hotel provided first class accommodation both for families and commercial travellers. The grounds, which covered one acre, contained tennis courts and a bowling green as well as stables and coach-house. In 1910 a large part of the property was demolished to widen the approach to Cobholm, Mill Road (earlier known as Love Lane) being a very narrow roadway between the Bear and the RAILWAY TAVERN (renamed the Rocket shortly after the closure of the station in 1970), a scheme the local residents had been petitioning for since 1889.

The Anchor and Hope, a favourite haunt of fishermen and boatmen.The Pier Hotel now stands on this site.

The ANSON ARMS was built by Samuel Paget, the Yarmouth brewer, in 1814, the original house being on the opposite side of the road to the present day public house. This and the nearby RUMBOLD ARMS (established before 1846) take their names from the two parliamentary candidates who fought many elections in the early part of the 19th century, representing the town many times in Parliament. At this time only freemen could vote at an election and there was much bribery and corruption when voters were encouraged to support a particular candidate.

The ANGEL or GUARDIAN ANGEL was owned by Pagets brewery in 1819 and drew much of its trade from the workers at the nearby Combe's Maltings and country folk coming into Southtown. Stables were available for 20 horses and several carriers called on their journey from Lowestoft to Yarmouth. It was rebuilt in 1842 and became the property of Steward, Patteson and Finch in 1845 when they took over Pagets brewery. In 1882 the old building was demolished and the new house was called the HALFWAY HOUSE, being the halfway point for the horse-trams from Yarmouth Bridge to Gorleston. This public house closed in September 1968 and was demolished a few months later as part of a road widening scheme.

Standing on the boundary of Southtown and Gorleston, where High Road becomes High Street, was the RISING SUN INN. This was another Pagets house, becoming the property of Steward Patteson and Finch in 1845. The Rising Sun closed in 1903 and the licence was transferred to the new STATION HOTEL in Lowestoft Road which had opened with the railway. On the opposite side of the road to the Rising Sun was the THREE TUNS, a Lacons house until it closed in 1942.

The GEORGE AND DRAGON in the High Street was a Lacons house from 1875 until it closed in 1925 when the licence was transferred to the new KEVILL ARMS.

The TRAMWAY HOTEL took its name from the nearby terminus of the horse-trams and was built to accommodate guests brought to Gorleston by the trams in the early days of the holiday industry. It was built on the site of an earlier public house called the HORSE AND GROOM, demolished soon after 1870. From 1903 until 1913 the Tramway was renowned for its 'sea pie supper', a meal held annually at which 50 diners consumed a pie weighing 2 cwt, 4 feet in length and 3 feet high. Land at the side of the Tramway, now the car park and doctor's surgery, were laid out as tennis courts in 1921 by the Surrey Lodge Tennis Club. The Tramway was completely destroyed by a direct hit during an air raid in June 1941, the occupants being killed. The owners, Diver and Sons, erected a temporary building on the site in 1948 and rebuilt the hotel in 1956.

The present WILLIAM IV in Beach Road was erected by Bullards Brewery in 1904 to replace an earlier house of the same name that had stood further to the west. This earlier public house was destroyed by fire in 1881. The William IV was the terminus for the horse-trams until the track was later extended to the Pavilion.

The Sefton Arms public house stood in Sefton Lane, Southtown

The PIER HOTEL stands on the site of an early public house called the ANCHOR AND HOPE, a popular rendezvous with the local beachmen and fishermen. In 1929 a Winter Garden was opened at the Pier Hotel to give the guests the benefit of "the finest lounge on the East Coast". Afternoon teas were served all year and the room had a maple dance floor, very different from the Anchor and Hope. The Pier was also a Lacons house and closed in 1940 for the duration of the war, like many other public houses.

The LINKS HOTEL on Marine Parade opened in April 1939 to serve the increasing population in the southern part of Gorleston. The licence for this house came from the Wheel of Fortune in George Street, Great Yarmouth which was closed.

Feathers Plain is one of the oldest parts of Gorleston, the site of early markets and fairs, and the FEATHERS INN is one of the oldest public houses in the town. The front was rebuilt in 1870. At one time the next building to the north was also a public house, the FISHING BOAT TAVERN.

Gorleston Police Firemen in the 1880s.

This booklet has only been able to outline the story of Southtown and Gorleston, and then only the recent centuries. The introduction has already mentioned the parallel publication *'Great Yarmouth - History, Herrings and Holidays'*. The story of the Gorleston lifeboat *Elizabeth Simpson* is recorded in another such booklet. Some other publications from Poppyland Publishing carry more detailed information. *'Great Yarmouth at War'* and *'The Rows of Great Yarmouth'* are currently available and new titles are in preparation.